MINE SHALL BE DONE

Mine Shall Be Done

Apostle Dr. Victor Adewusi

Apostle Dr. Victor Adewusi Foundation

Contents

Copyright vi
Foreword vii

1. You Need Faith — 1
2. Are You Convinced? — 5
3. Some Specific Miracles of God and Their Implications — 18
4. The Final Leg — 29
5. The Place of Nows, Pledges & Appreciation — 33
6. Sin, the Master Stopper! — 37
7. Family Generational Curses — 40
8. The Golden Steps to Answered Prayers — 42

A Sinner's Prayer 45
About the Author 47

Copyright © 2022 by Aposle Dr. Victor Adewusi

All rights reserved. No part of this book may be used or reproduced by any means, graphics, electronic, or mechanical, including photocopying, recording, taping or by any information storage retrieval system without the author's written permission except in cases of brief quotations embodied in critical articles and reviews.

Scripture quotations marked NLT are taken from the New Living Translation. Copyright © 1996, 2004, 2007 by Tyndale House Foundation. Used by permission of Tyndale House Publishers, Inc., Carol Stream, Illinois 60188. All rights reserved.

Author: Apostle Dr. Victor Adewusi

ISBN: 978-1-989099-17-9 (hardcover)
ISBN: 978-1-989099-16-2 (ebook)

First Printing, 2022

Foreword

I count it an immense privilege to write the foreword for this extraordinary book. The deceased author, who was also my father, was well qualified to write a book of this kind as a result of the extraordinary faith he demonstrated. This is a book about faith in God and will challenge you to grow your faith in God to a higher level.

As the third child in the family, I saw firsthand over thirty years of tenacity, doggedness, grit, determination, and sheer faith in the divine. I could tell story after story of how the author lived out his faith in the midst of myriads of challenges. Certainly, like most other families, we experienced health challenges, financial challenges, social challenges, and spiritual challenges, to name a few. I will focus the lens of this foreword on the words and action perspective of a faith-filled life.

Faith is primarily demonstrated through words and action. Anyone who knew my father would attest to his meticulous use of words. To dad, words were not just a means of communication with fellow humans but also with our environment and the spiritual realm. Dad was very particular about saying what you mean and meaning what you say. You could not hang around him without getting corrected about your words. I remember an incident where an elder was asking after dad's younger brother, whose name translates to "joy." In asking about dad's younger brother in Yoruba, the elder's question translated into him saying, "Has joy left?" Dad immediately responded in a respectful way, saying, "Joy is still here, but my younger brother has left." The elder immediately understood what dad was saying and adjusted accordingly. Dad wasn't only all talk, though.

Dad had the action to match his meticulous choice of words. I saw dad pursue audacious goals even when the resources were not available at the time. I saw how dad applied the force of prayer and fasting to bring to pass on earth what has been established in heaven. Dad hardly took no for an answer. In response to receiving a not-so-good grade, dad would often respond by saying, "those that took first place don't have two heads." In essence, he was saying, if they could do it, why not me? Impossibility was not in dad's dictionary. Dad not only demonstrated his faith by his actions, but he also inspired others to do the same. After his transition to glory, many stories have emerged from people who have been inspired to press on and make lemonade with the lemons in their possession.

As you read this book, may the power of the Holy Spirit empower you to stand your ground when life's challenges come bellowing. May you be empowered to reach for the very top and never settle for less. In Jesus' name, every of God's promises over your life will come to pass.

Emmanuel Adewusi

1

You Need Faith

The inspiration to write this book fell upon me whenever I was alone, and I began to constantly ruminate over the various miracles that were performed by God and, by extension, the ones that were done by our Dear Lord and Personal Savior, Jesus Christ of Nazareth, during the 3 1/2 reign of His Ministry.

Secondly, I suddenly realized that perhaps due to the negative impacts of the global pandemic (Covid-19), many people were becoming demoralized in one way or the other due to one catastrophe or the other, notably:

1. **Dwindling fortunes**
2. **Loss of jobs**
3. **Loss of a relative**
4. **Loss of a breadwinner**
5. **Disability due to health challenges**
6. **Business closures**

Thirdly, it dawned on me that the worldwide pandemic notwithstanding, most economies of the world were already experiencing depression of varying forms, which unavoidably encourages job cuts, job losses and the devaluation of countries' currencies.

Therefore, people are now running from pillar to post and helter-skelter, looking for solutions at all costs. Many people attempt to run to friends, colleagues, associates, family members, occultists, herbalists and even soothsayers in order to be bailed out. Others look up to their church pastors and imams/sheiks for succour, while some even expect their parents to bail them out.

Among all of the expected solution providers listed above, NONE could be compared to the ONLY Solution Master Himself, the King of Kings and the Lord of Lords, who is Jesus Christ of Nazareth. And that was what propelled me to sit down and present to you, my numerous readers, and the simple analysis of the pungent breakdown of some of the uncountable miracles that Jesus Christ of Nazareth performed.

I am thoroughly convinced that if we can sincerely, religiously and dedicatedly sit down to read, chew, analyze and believe in them by applying them to our life situations, ultimate success shall become ours at the end of the day. We can only ever discuss some of them because not ALL of the miracles performed by Jesus Christ of Nazareth were recorded in the Bible, according to John 20:30 - "And many other signs Jesus did in the presence of His Disciples, which are not written in this Book" (i.e. the Bible).

Before we begin to highlight and discuss them, I wish to show you quickly, my readers, some of the major Golden [scripture] Verses upon which I solely believe the Book and the narrations are based upon, v.z:

1. **Jeremiah 32:27** - *"Behold, I am the Lord, the God of all flesh: is there anything too hard for me?"*

2. **Mark 9:23** - *"Jesus said unto him if thou can believe, all things are possible to him that believes."*
3. **Luke 1:37** - *"For with God, nothing shall be impossible."*
4. **Mark 11:22-24** - *"And Jesus answering said unto them, Have faith in God. For verily I say unto you, That whosoever shall say unto the mountain, be removed, and be thou cast into the sea; and shall not doubt in his heart, but shall believe that those things which he said shall come to pass, he shall have whatsoever he said. Therefore I say unto you, whatsoever things ye desire, when ye pray, believe that ye receive them, and ye shall have them."*
5. **Isaiah 55:11** - *"So shall my Word be that goeth of My mouth; it shall not return unto Me void, but it shall accomplish that which I please, and it shall prosper in the thing whereto I sent it."*
6. **Malachi 3:6a** - *"I am the Lord, I change not."*
7. **Hebrews 11:6** - *"But without faith, it is impossible to please Him; for he that cometh to God must believe that He is and that He is a Rewarder of them that diligently seek Him."*
8. **Romans 3:3** - *"For what if some did not believe? Shall their unbelief make the faith of God without effect?"*
9. **Matthew 24:35** - *"Heaven and the Earth shall pass away, but My Words shall not pass away."*
10. **2 Timothy 2:13** - *"If we believe not, yet He abideth faithful; He cannot deny Himself."*
11. **Hebrews 3:12** - *"Take heed, brethren, lest there be any of you an evil heart of unbelief, in departing from the Living God."*
12. **I John 4:1** - *"Beloved, believe not every spirit, but try the spirit whether they are of God because many false prophets are gone out unto the world."*
13. **Mark 4:40** - *"And He said unto them, Why are ye so fearful? How is it that ye have no faith?"*

14. **Deuteronomy 32:20** - *"And He said I will hide my face from them, I will see what their end shall be; for they are a very forward generation, children in whom is no faith."*
15. **Isaiah 7:9b** - *"If ye will not believe, surely ye shall not be established."*
16. **James 1:6-7** - *"But let them ask in faith, nothing wavering. For he that wavereth is like a wave of the sea driven with the wind and tossed. For let not that man think that he shall receive anything of the Lord."*
17. **Isaiah 58:8- 9** - *"For My thoughts are not your thoughts, neither are your ways My ways, saith the Lord. For as the heavens are higher than the Earth, so are My ways higher than your ways; and My thoughts than your thoughts."*
18. **John 20:29** - *"Jesus said unto him, Thomas, because thou Lest seen Me, though has believed; blessed are they that have not seen Me, and yet have believed."*
19. **2 Peter 1:16-19** - *"For we have not followed cunningly devised fables when we made known to you the power and coming of our Lord Jesus Christ, but we were eyewitnesses of His Majesty. We also have a more sure Word of prophecy, whereunto ye do well that ye take heed, as unto a light that shineth in a dark place, until the day dawn, and the day star arise in your hearts."*
20. **2 Chronicles 20:20b** - *"Believe in the Lord your God, so shall ye be established; believe His prophets, so shall ye prosper."*
21. **Romans 5:1** - *"Therefore being justified by faith, we have peace with God through our Lord, Jesus Christ."*

2

Are You Convinced?

From the Bible references cited above, we can vividly confirm that once we have unflinching faith in God, it is very easy for our needs to be met, especially if we combine our faith with constant prayers and walk in alignment with God. Remember that according to Genesis 37:23-28, Joseph was thrown into the pit, but he still shone. Therefore, if we believe that we serve a living God, we can achieve every objective in life by running with our dreams without looking back, whether the devil likes it or not.

Consider the Following

In mathematics, we call some things "CONSTANTS." Meaning, that if we want to solve some mathematical issues, some indices have to be held permanently. For instance, we usually say that if a=b and b=c, then a=c. Similarly, the following could be regarded as some of the "Biblical Constants"; therefore, it implies that if we can embrace them, it would be very easy for us to achieve our aims and objectives in life.

According to **Ecclesiastes 9:4**, as long as you are still alive, there is hope for you because a living dog is better than a dead lion.

Joseph was sold into slavery while he was in the house of Potiphar, but he still became No.2 in Egypt, according to **Genesis 39:1-6**.

2 Timothy 2:13 - Even if we don't believe Him, He remains Faithful.

Genesis 17:1 - His Name is Jehovah El-Shaddai meaning the All-Sufficient God.

I John 4:8 - He loves us because His Name is love.

Romans 8:31-32 - He loves us by giving us His Only Begotten Son.

Psalm 94:9 - He who created the eyes can see, and He who created the ears can hear.

Psalm 30:11 - When God pays you a visit, He turns mourning to dancing.

Isaiah 43:13 - God says when I am ready to do something, who can stop me?

Genesis 1:26-28 - God says human beings should be fruitful and multiply.

Haggai 2:8 - God says all the Silver and the Gold in this world belong to Him.

Psalm 50:15 - God says we should call unto Him in the day of trouble; He will deliver us, and we shall glorify Him.

Psalm 30:5 - Weeping may endure for a night, but joy cometh in the morning.

Isaiah 43:20 - God gives water in the wilderness and rivers in the desert to give to His chosen Ones.

John 8:36 - Whomever the Son, [that is] Jesus sets free, shall be free indeed.

Deuteronomy 28:13 - We shall be the head and not the tail.

Deuteronomy 28:7 - Enemies and detractors will pursue or attack us once, but we shall defeat them seven times.

Genesis 18:1-14 - God remembered Abraham and Sarah even in their old age.

John 11:35-40 - The power that raised Lazarus from the dead is very much alive.

Psalm 33:8-9 - Once God speaks, it is done.

Psalm 75:6-7 - Promotion does not come from the East, West, South, or the North but from God.

Mark 9:23 - If we can believe, all things are possible with God.

Mark 11:22-23 - Once we believe, we can move mountains.

Luke 1:37 - With God, all things are possible.

Jeremiah 32:27 - Behold, I am the God of all flesh; is there anything too difficult for me to do?

John 6:5-13 - God (Jesus Christ) made a boy surrender his pack of food, which He used to feed multitudes.

Psalm 115:3 - Our God is in Heaven, doing what He pleases, and nobody can query Him.

Romans 8:32 - If God really loves us and He gave His Only-begotten Son, what else can He not do?

Numbers 23:19 - God is not a man that He should lie.

Jeremiah 33:3 - God says we should call on Him, and He will show us great things that we did not know before.

Isaiah 10:12-13 - Joshua commanded the Sun and the Moon to stand still over Gibeon in the Valley of Aijalon.

Exodus 12:35-36 - Everything that the Israelites had lost in 450 yrs was recovered in less than 24 hrs.

John 14:6 - Jesus Christ is the Way, the Life and the Truth.

Hebrews 12:29 - Our God is a Consuming Fire.

Joel 2:24 - God says He will restore to us the years that we have missed, and we shall not be ashamed.

Isaiah 10:27 - Yokes shall be destroyed by the anointing.

Psalm 105:14 - Touch not my anointed, and do my prophets no harm.

I Kings 19:1-8 - Only God has the last say about our lives.

Judges 6:15 - Gideon said he is a small man from a small family from a small village, but God said I will use you.

2 Chronicles 16:9 - The eyes of the Lord runs throughout the whole world.

Romans 8:31 - If God be for us, who can be against us?

I Corinthians 10:13 - There is no temptation that can come to us that we cannot handle. God will provide a way out. Hence, temptations are graded.

John 3:16 - For God so loved the world that He sent His only begotten Son, that whosoever believes in Him will not perish, but have everlasting life.

Zechariah 4:6 - It is not by power or might, but by My spirit.

Psalm 46:1 - Jesus Christ is the Ever-present help in times of trouble

Proverbs 18:10 - The Name of the Lord is a Strong Tower, the righteous run into it, and he is saved.

Isaiah 9:6 - Jesus is the Prince of Peace.

Mark 4:39-41 - The wind, air and the storms of life obey Him because he is the Prince of Peace!

Luke 8:22-24 - Whenever He stills any storm, such storm does not rise again.

Mark 4: 39-41 - Whatever He has done before, He can do it again. But if He is not in any ship, it would sink.

John 14:12 - Jesus says if you believe in Me, you will do greater things than I have done.

Ecclesiastes 7:8 - Better is the end of a thing than the beginning.

Proverbs 4:18 - The path of the righteous keeps shining.

Galatians 3:9 - Every Christian is a seed of Abraham.

Jeremiah 29:11 - God has good plans for us and created us for something big.

Proverbs 10:28 - The hope of the righteous shall flourish.

Psalm 150:6 - Let everything that has breath praise the Lord.

Colossians 2:15 - Jesus Christ fought all principalities and powers.

Isaiah 42:10 - God will always give us a new song.

Romans 10:17 - Faith comes by hearing and hearing by the Word of God.

Mark 1: 23-26 - Even in the Church, there are various challenges.

2 Corinthians 5:7 - We don't walk by sight but by faith.

Revelation 4:11 - God created us for His pleasure; He has no pleasure in the death of sinners.

Psalm 33:10-11 - All the devices of the devil shall be brought to nought.

Isaiah 64:8 - God is the Potter; we are the clay.

Exodus 3:13-14 - God's Name is I am that I am.

I Samuel 2: 7-8 - God has the power to raise, promote and bring down.

Proverbs 21:1 - The heart of the King is in the hand of God.

Hebrew 7:25 - The power to save to the uttermost belongs to God.

Matthew 28:18 - All powers on Earth and in Heaven have been given to me.

Deuteronomy 32:39 - God has the ability to kill and make alive.

Philippians 4:13 - I can do all things through Christ who strengthens me.

Romans 8:37 - We are more than conquerors through Christ, who strengthens me.

Psalm 23:5 - The Lord prepares a table before me, in the presence of my enemies.

Hosea 4:6 - My People perish for lack of knowledge.

Revelation 3:11 - Hold fast that which you have, lest nobody take away your crown.

Matthew 6:24 - You cannot serve two Masters.

Acts 2:21 - Behold, whoever calls upon the Name of the Lord shall be saved.

Ecclesiastes 5:9 - Everything beneficial to Man comes from the ground.

Proverbs 13:22 - God has laid up so much for us that even our Grandchildren can eat out of the surplus.

I Samuel 15:22 - Obedience is better than sacrifice.

John 15:16 - Jesus said, you have not chosen Me, I chose you.

I Corinthians 6:19 - Our body is the temple of God.

Psalm 86:15 - God is full of compassion.

Ephesians 6:12-17 - We fight principalities, power and the devil.

Matthew 14:29 - Jesus suspended the Law of Gravity for them to walk on water.

Matthew 8:16 - Jesus Christ casts out the devil with His Word.

2 Corinthians 9:6 - Sow bountifully and reap bountifully.

Psalm 16:11 - In the presence of God, there is fullness (plenty) of joy.

John 16:24 - Jesus Christ says ask till your joy is full.

Psalm 16:4 - The sorrows of those that follow lower gods shall be plenty.

Ephesians 3:20 - God is able to do abundantly and exceedingly above all of our expectations.

Isaiah 3:10 - Say ye to the righteous that it shall be well with him.

Exodus 14:1-31 - There will always be a Red Sea to pass before getting to your Promise Land because the devil will always want to cross your path to glory.

John 11:38-44 - Whenever God speaks, everything hears: the Sun, Moon, Stars, Blacks and Whites.

Matthew 19:26 - With Men, this is impossible, but with God, all things are possible.

Matthew 17:20 - Jesus Christ says if we have faith like a mustard seed, we shall command mountains to move, and nothing shall be impossible.

Proverbs 10:22 - The blessings of the Lord maketh rich and addeth no sorrow.

Philippians 1:6 - Once God begins something, He will complete it.

Deuteronomy 15:4 - The poor shall not cease from the land.

Mark 12:30-31 - Love the Lord with all your heart.

Philippians 4:7 - The peace of God that passeth all understanding.

I John 1:7 - The Blood of Jesus washes away all our sins.

Revelation 12:10-11 - His Blood gives us victory over satan.

Luke 4:25-26 - There were many Widows in Israel in the days of Elijah, but God knew that the widow of Zarephath was the only one that would meet the need of Elijah.

I Thessalonians 5:17-19 - We must pray without ceasing.

Job 14:7-10 - There is hope for a tree.

2 Corinthians 8:9 - Jesus Christ became poor so that we can become rich.

I Peter 2:24 - By His stripes, you were healed.

Matthew 15:13 - Every plant that my Father has not planted shall be uprooted.

Matthew 10:26 - Nothing is hidden that will not come to the open.

Proverbs 15:8 - The sacrifice of the wicked is an abomination to God.

Amos 3:3 - How can two people walk together unless they agree?

I Kings 8:36 - Elijah asked God to prove Himself, and fire came down.

Ecclesiastes 5:4 - When you make a vow, don't delay to redeem it.

Mark 10:22 - What is impossible with man is possible with God.

Psalm 50:15 - Call on me on the day of trouble, and I will answer you.

Habakkuk 2:24, Romans 1:17, Galatians 3:11, Hebrews 10:38 - The just shall live by faith.

I Samuel 16:11-13 - Samuel was the Destiny Helper sent to David because David's family had written him off.

Psalm 27:10 - When my father and mother forsake me, then the Lord will take me up.

Psalm 106:8 - He will do it for His Name's sake.

Matthew 15:21-28 - Jesus Christ said He could not give the bread of man to dogs.

I Samuel 2:7 - You cannot query God.

Esther 6:1-13 - Haman wanted to destroy Mordecai, but God did not allow King Ahasuerus to sleep.

Revelation 3:7 - God said I have the key to David; when I open, nobody can shut, and when I shut, nobody can open.

Psalm 33:4 - The counsel of the Lord shall stand because He has the final say.

Isaiah 45:11 - God says I am the Holy One of Israel; concerning the works of my hand, command Me.

Genesis 26:12-14 - When God blessed Isaac during the famine, the Philistines envied him because he was lending to Nations.

Deuteronomy 33:40 - God never lies.

Joshua 6:20 - The wall of Jericho collapsed and fell down.

Isaiah 54:15 - Surely they will gather but not by My knowledge.

John 15:16 - You are my friend if you do what I command you.

Jeremiah 17:5-8 - If you put your trust in men, you are wasting your time.

Job 36:11-18 - If they obey and serve Me, they will spend their years in plenty.

Genesis 32:1-6 - Despite Esau losing his birthright and his father's blessings to his younger brother Jacob, he still prospered, as evidenced by his having approximately 400 bodyguards.

John 6:5-13 - 5 fishes and two loaves of bread.

Proverbs 10:15 - Poverty is a destroyer.

Isaiah.14:12-17 - Satan always wants to prove that it rules in the affairs of Men.

A common thread that runs through all of the above is the importance of constant faith and shows the following:

1. **We must totally rely on God.**
2. **He has the power to do all things.**
3. **We must never waver; we do this by depending on Him entirely.**
4. **Once we dedicatedly rely on Him, practically nothing is impossible for Him to do.**
5. **Once He promises to do something, He will do it because He never lies.**
6. **Everybody needs a Destiny Helper.**
7. **We must never put our trust in Man, only in God.**
8. **God is kind and full of compassion.**

3

Some Specific Miracles of God and Their Implications

Now, having cited all the above as "templates and major foundations" for this book, please join me as I explore some of the major miracles performed by God (and by extension, through Jesus Christ of Nazareth and other Vessels) as recorded in the Bible.

1. We all know that Jesus Christ earlier prophesied that He would rise on the 3rd day after His death, but many people never believed Him. That is why heavy stones were kept at the entrance of His tomb, to ensure that even if He arose as prophesied, it would be practically impossible for Him to come out. NOT only that, many stern-looking soldiers were stationed at the entrance of the tomb. But what happened? He rose on the 3rd day exactly as He prophesied, and the stones were glaringly rolled away! If that wasn't already a shocker, please wait for this because you might not have thought about it or realized it: When they peeped into His tomb, the sackcloth was left inside the tomb. And the

great shocker? While He was ascending into Heaven, He did not go unclad or naked; He had a garment on! Who sewed it? How did He come about it? What a mystery!

I decree that as from today, the miraculous Hand that covered the nakedness of Jesus Christ of Nazareth will forever continue to cover your shame, provide for you, take you to greater heights and confound your detractors by His Grace.

Similarly, the Unseen Hand and the force that effortlessly rolled away all of the stones used at the entrance of Jesus Christ's tomb shall consistently remove all of the impediments to your glory, breakthrough, progress, joy, and upliftments in Jesus Christ's Name, Amen.

2. In **Exodus 9:22-26**, Moses called on fire and brimstone to fall upon the Egyptians. Though the Israelites were there, the fire and brimstones did not affect them because they were stationed in Goshen (Verse 26). I decree today, wherever there is confusion, chaos and any form of calamity, it shall not come near you nor any of your loved ones, especially according to Psalm 91, 46 and 125, in Jesus Christ's Name.

3. In **Exodus 14:21-31**, the Egyptians attacked the Israelites and pursued them up to the Red Sea. God instructed Moses to stretch his rod towards the Red Sea, and He sent wind from the east, and The Red Sea parted. The Children of Israel walked on dry land, and not a single soul among the Israelites was affected. However, all of the Chariots of Pharaoh and Pharaoh himself were drowned in the Red Sea because it opened upon them from the first person to the last person among the Egyptians.

Every negative issue that has been pursuing us in one way or another shall be consumed by the East wind, and you will see them no more.

4. In **Exodus 15:23-25**, the Israelites had just miraculously escaped from the Red Sea now approaching Zur and were panting, as they were unavoidably thirsty and in need of water; however, the water they encountered was bitter, and in turn, they decided to name it Marah -meaning bitter. God told Moses to cast a piece of a tree into the water, and the bitterness disappeared.

As of today, every form of bitterness in any area of your lives shall be turned to sweetness by God's Grace.

5. In **Exodus 16:12-17**, relying on what God did by providing water for them, the Children of Israel told Moses that they wanted to eat meat. Moses was initially furious because he felt that they were asking for the impossible! Nonetheless, he stepped aside and told God about the request of the Israelites; God said that they would eat meat.

Not too long after delivering God's message to them, the same wind from the East blew; lo and behold, manna began to fall from heaven within reach of the Israelites. They caught the manna with ease and ate to their satisfaction.

I decree that from today, whatever you want God to do for you, He will place them in your palms with ease and comfort by His abundant Grace.

6. In **Joshua 3:14-17**, the people of Israel were still marching to the Promised Land, and when they got to Jordan, Moses stretched out his staff, and the river parted, thereby enabling them to cross with ease.

Whatever wants to act as a stumbling block to your progress shall suddenly crumble by God's Grace.

7. In **Ezekiel 37:1-14**, God called and took Ezekiel to the Valley of the dry bones and asked Ezekiel if the dry bones could resurrect by coming back to life again. Of course, Ezekiel was very wise, and instead of saying "Yes" or "No," he answered God that it was Him alone that could decide or ascertain if the dry bones could come back to life again. Eventually, the dry bones rose again, to the pleasant surprise of everyone and the whole of Israel.

I prophesy into your life that since Jesus Christ is the same yesterday, today and forever, according to Hebrews 13:8, that same power that raised the dry bones to life shall touch all the dead bones of your life and cause every dead aspect of your life to receive life by His Grace.

8. In **Exodus 17:1-7**, While the Children of Israel were moving through the wilderness, they arrived at Rephidim and became thirsty again. They began to harass Moses ceaselessly, making Moses cry unto the Lord about what he should do. God told him to take his rod and three of the Elders with him to Horeb and once there to stand upon a rock. The exact place was Massah, in Meribah. Moses did as the Lord had directed him, and water came out of the rock for the Children of Israel to drink.

May God continue to provide for our immediate needs in a miraculous manner; because if water could come out of the rock in the wilderness, there is nothing that He cannot do.

9. In **Joshua 6:6-20**, the Children of Israel were on their way to the Promised Land under the leading of Joshua - the son of Nun. When they arrived at Jericho, they could not move forward with the Ark of Covenant; so Joshua instructed them to march around the city once for six days in silence and, on the seventh day, to march around the city seven times, releasing a shout once they heard the sound of the trumpets. They did as instructed, and the wall of Jericho fell down flat.

10. In **I Kings 17**, God told Elijah the Tishbite that rain would cease for the next three years, indicating that there would be famine in the land. And because God did not want Elijah to starve, He directed him to go Eastward of Israel and hide there by the Brook of Cherish, before Jordan. God instructed Elijah to drink from the brook, and at the same spot, He would command the Ravens to supply him with bread and fish both in the morning and evening.

It continued unabated until the Brook dried up because there was no rain in the land. And again, God did not want Elijah to starve, so He directed him again, but this time to a particular widowed woman in Zarephath with one child. Elijah met the Woman at the point where she was going to fetch food for herself and her only son; and told her first to prepare a meal for him. However, the Widow said she only had a handful of flour and a bit of oil left that she was about to prepare so that they could eat it and die.

Elijah nonetheless impressed upon her not to fear but to prepare a meal for him and see what God would do thereafter. She complied, and as a result of her obedience, her miracles began. Elijah instructed her to lock herself in the room, borrow as many empty bottles of oil as possible and begin to turn the containers of the empty oil into those drums/barrels. One after the other, the drums filled up until there were no more remaining for oil to be poured into. The Woman became rich, popular, prosperous and never suffered throughout the rest of the famine and beyond.

During Elijah's stay, her only Son became sick and died, and she brought questions to Elijah, asking him if he came to bring remembrance to her sin, to kill her son. In response, Elijah asked for her son and took him to the upper room of the widow's house that she prepared for his stay during the famine and cried out to the Lord. He stretched himself out on the boy three times, and when the Lord heard his cries, the boy sneezed and came back to life.

The moral of the lessons above has aptly described the title of this book in a gigantic manner. They have all shown that with God, all things are possible once we put our faith to work, without wavering in any form.

11. Elisha, the Prophet (who took over from Elijah after the Chariots took him to heaven), was on his way to Jericho when the sons of the Prophets saw him. They urged him to do something about the bitterness of the water in the land, and he promptly directed them to bring a new bowl with salt in it. After praying, he poured it into the waters of the land, and the bitterness turned sweet and drinkable instantly. The lesson here is that with God's unction of the Holy Spirit, coupled with one's faith, nothing shall be impossible before God.

The event above was not the end of Elisha's miracles. As he was on his way to another place, he met the sons of prophets who then dwelled with him. As their dwelling place became too small, the sons asked Elisha if they could go to Jordan for beams to build a small tent for their habitation. As they were cutting down the trees, the axe head fell into the water, and they began lamenting that the axe was borrowed. Elisha the prophet asked the men to show him where the axe had fallen, then took a piece of wood, and as he threw it into the water, the iron began to float and was brought out.

That was another miracle by God through Elisha, depicting that with Him, nothing shall be impossible. Otherwise, how can we rationalize that a piece of light wood could sink to the bottom of the water and a heavy piece of iron could, in turn, float to the surface? Only the hand of God could have done that!

12. Elisha was a very great prophet of the Most High God. For this reason, I wish to expound on some of the other fascinating miracles that God performed through him. **2 Kings 5:1-28** tells us about the story of Naaman, who was a very senior Military Officer in the Army of Syria. He was a leper and went to several places before to receive healing without success. The King of Syria gave him a letter of recommendation for the King of Israel, which he took along with ten talents of silver, six thousand pieces of gold and ten raiments as gifts for his healing.

However, when the King of Israel read the letter, he was greatly annoyed and tore his clothes, saying, *"Am I God, to kill and to destroy and heal a man of leprosy?"* When Elisha heard about the matter, he sent for Naaman, who then went with his horses and chariots to the door of Elisha's house. Elisha didn't invite him in, nor did he go outside of his domain to attend to him. Instead, he sent one of his servants to instruct Naaman to wash himself in the Jordan seven times. Naaman became greatly annoyed and wanted to disobey the instructions of Elisha. Not only did he have the wrong expectation that Elisha would come out to heal him, but he also looked down upon the river Jordan commenting: *"Are not the Abana and the Pharpar, the rivers of Damascus, better than all the waters of Israel? Could I not wash in them and be clean?"* Through the encouragement of his servants to do as the man of God instructed him, he dipped into the river seven times, and leprosy disappeared with his flesh being restored like the flesh of a little child.

The moral of this lesson is? We should not look down on anybody or anything, as God can use any person or manner to perform miracles if we have faith and are not proud.

13. **Daniel 3:19-27** tells us about the unforgettable account of King Nebuchadnezzar, king of Babylon and 3 Jews. The king made a decree that everyone who heard the sound of the horn, flute, harp, lyre and

psaltery in symphony should bow down before the golden image or otherwise be cast into the fiery furnace. The three Jewish men: Shadrach, Meshach, and Abed-Nego, disobeyed the decree by their refusal to bow down before the golden image.

The King became furious and commanded his men to heat the furnace seven times hotter than usual and to bind the three men and cast them into the burning furnace after they did not waver when challenged by the king directly. It was recorded in the Bible that not only were the three men unharmed, but to the king's astonishment, when he looked into the furnace, he saw four men loose and walking amid the fire instead of three whom he had previously bound together. Apparently, the 4th Man was the King of Kings, Jesus Christ of Nazareth, who turned the hot and burning furnace into an Air-Condition!

It is, however, important to note that those who attempted to throw the 3 Jews into the burning furnace were burnt to ashes. When the King saw that the 3 Men came out unscathed, he promoted them in the Province of Babylon and decreed that henceforth, whoever failed to serve the God Of Shadrach, Meshach, and Abednego should be cut into pieces.

14. As we continue in the book of **Daniel 6:16-20**, we'll come upon the vivid account of Daniel, who was thrown into the den of lions.

King Darius had 120 Princes in charge of the Province, but Daniel was the most senior to whom the majority of the people reported to because of his wisdom and excellent spirit. But a decree was passed that for 30 days, nobody should pray to any God again, except they bow down before a royal statue. They saw that Daniel did not obey the decree when he opened his window and began to pray. Daniel was summoned, and upon interrogation, he did not deny his God. The King ordered that he should be thrown into the den of lions saying, *"Your God, whom you serve continually, He will deliver you."* A stone was then placed on the mouth of the den and sealed with the king's signet ring and that of his lord, signifying that the verdict against Daniel would remain unchanged. That night, the king was unable to sleep and arose early the following morning and hurriedly went to the den of lions and said to Daniel: *"Daniel, servant of the living God, has your God, whom you serve continually, been able to deliver you from the lions?"* Daniel responded, *"O king, live forever! My God sent His angel and shut the lions' mouths so that they have not hurt me because I was found innocent before Him; and also, O king, I have done no wrong before you."* Relieved, the king commanded that Daniel be removed from the den and found that he sustained no injuries whatsoever! In turn, the king commanded those who accused Daniel to be thrown into the den of lions along with their households, where they were eventually overpowered by the lions. The king then made a decree that each person in his kingdom must tremble and fear before the God of Daniel.

15. In **Acts 9:36-42**, Tabitha (meaning Dorcas), one of the many followers of Jesus Christ, became sick and eventually died. She was washed and then laid in her upper room. She was well known In Joppa for her good works, humanitarian deeds and good character, and because of this, the news of her death touched many people. When the other followers caught wind of the news that Peter was in the same town, they sent two men to tell him about her. Peter went with them, and in the upper room, he knelt beside her corpse and prayed. Turning toward her, he said, *"Tabitha, arise,"* and when she opened her eyes and saw Peter, she sat up. He then stretched his hand, and she stood up.

The takeaway is that God used the case of Tabitha (Dorcas) to propagate the Gospel of Jesus Christ in the City and her neighbourhood; because this miracle became known throughout Joppa, many people then believed in the Lord. Thus, nobody and nothing can hinder God from performing His miracles whenever it is time to do anything major in our lives.

16. It was reported in Acts of the **Apostles 14:8-11** that Paul was preaching in Lystra when one of his listeners, who was born lame from his mother's womb, heard his sermon, and because of his belief, he was healed and began to walk instantly.

Whatever might have been crawling in our lives will miraculously receive prompt healing as from today, in Jesus Christ's Name.

17. A woman had the spirit of divination, according to **Acts of the Apostles 16:16-18**. Paul commanded the negative spirit to leave her, and although it disappeared immediately, the miracle did not go down well with the people. They arranged for Paul and Silas to be arrested and imprisoned and beat them severely with many stripes while being bound hands and feet in chains before their imprisonment.

However, instead of being downcast, Paul and Silas began praying and singing praises unto the Lord at midnight. These songs of praise not only caused their chains to loose, but the foundations of the prison began to shake, and the prison doors opened. The prison keeper awoke in surprise, so much so that he drew his sword to commit suicide, but Paul cried out to him that he should not kill himself since they did not escape. That singular miracle forced him to tremble and fall down before them and he sought to know what he should do to be saved. They told him to believe in Jesus Christ, and he and his household will be saved. He immediately washed their stripes in the midnight while they, in turn, baptized him and his entire household.

18. According to the book of **Mark 16:15-18**, before His ascension into heaven, Jesus Christ of Nazareth admonished His Disciples to go into the world and preach the gospel saying, *"He that believed and is baptized by the Holy Spirit shall be saved. Whoever does not believe shall be damned, and that these signs shall follow them that believe; in My Name shall*

they cast out demons, and they will speak with new tongues. They shall take up serpents, and if they drink any deadly thing, it shall not hurt them; they shall lay hands on the sick, and they shall recover."

I deliberately quoted the above as icing to safely seal our narration of how possible it is to receive our miracles once we believe and have faith in God as the ONLY One that can make all things possible for us.

4

The Final Leg

Let me begin to share with you other pungent areas of the Bible that vividly confirm that ours shall indeed be possible with God.

We must learn to trust in the Lord with all our hearts (Proverbs 3:5-6) because nothing is too hard for Him to do as long as we believe. (Jeremiah 32:27).

Even if we cannot think of anything about His mightiness, we must constantly think about His glory and greatness (I Chronicles 29:11-12) because He is the greatest Shepherd (Psalm 23). Additionally, He is our Everlasting light and salvation (Psalm 27) and our refuge and strength.

At every point in time, we must never forget that He calmed the storm on many occasions (Matthew 14:22-31, Mark 4:37-40); and know that He is faithful because His Mercies are new every morning (Lamentations 3:22-32). Once we can trust and delight in Him and wait patiently for Him (Psalm 37:1-7), there will be no reason for us to be downcast (Psalm 42:5).

Whether we believe it or not, He is very close to us and continues to guide us as long as we intuitively surrender our challenges entirely to

Him (Psalm 73:23-28). That is why He wants us to permanently put our hope and trust in Him (Isaiah 40:11-31) without being fearful (Isaiah 43:1-3, Isaiah 41:10). He encourages us to call upon Him daily with faith (Jeremiah 33:3, Psalm 50:15) because as long as He can provide for birds and ordinary flowers (Matthew 6:25-34), there is nothing that He cannot do for us, as His Image (Psalm 82:6, I John 4:4).

Two major ingredients we need as human beings are unwavering courage (Joshua 1:1-9) and unrepentant belief in His unfailing love (Isaiah 26:3-4, Nahum 1:7, Jeremiah 17:7-8, Isaiah 31:1, Psalm 46, 57, 9:9, 28:7-8). He will never allow anyone who relies on Him and fears Him to be disappointed (Psalm 33:18-22, Psalm 62:5-8) and cannot forget such people (Isaiah 49:14-16, Psalm 147:11, Psalm 13:5-6). And for those who do not trust in Him, He utterly rebukes them (Deuteronomy 1:26-36).

The Bible says that it is impossible to serve 2 Masters (Matthew 6:24); hence, our salvation comes through Jesus Christ alone (Acts 4:12, John 3:16, John 10:9, John 14:6). Remember that He is the Resurrection and the life (John 11:25-26, Acts 16:31, I John 5:1) we stand to receive answers to our requests from Him. More so, if we can destroy the works of the flesh (I Corinthians 5:5), then we shall have the assurance that He will never leave nor forsake us (2 Timothy 2:13).

In order for us to receive prompt answers to our prayer requests, we must imbibe the culture of applying His Words during prayer. He usually sends His Words to heal us and by extension to answer our supplications if we put our trust in His Words (Psalm 107:20, Psalm 119:89, Isaiah 55:10-11, Matthew 24:35, John 10:35, I Peter 1:25; as well as, Psalm 138:2, John 1:1-5, Revelation 19:11-13, John 6:63) because His Word is like fire (Jeremiah 23:29, Hebrew 4:12, Jeremiah 5:14).

Those who hear, use and obey God's Word are regularly blessed (Luke 11:28, Luke 8:15, Deuteronomy 7:9) because if we ask Him for anything, He will answer us with minimum delay (John 15:7). That is why we are enjoined to constantly meditate on His Words (Joshua 1:8), as He said Man shall not live by bread alone but by every word that proceeds out of His mouth (Matthew 4:4).

If we want God to make our supplications urgently or speedily possible, we must have unalloyed faith in Him (Matthew 17:20) just like the mustard seed because we walk by faith and not by sight (2 Corinthians 5:7). And without faith, it is impossible to please God (Hebrews 11:6) talkless of receiving something from Him.

Peter is an excellent example of someone who had faith in God's word and faithfulness. After toiling all night, Jesus Christ appeared to him and told him to throw his nets in a particular direction (Luke 5:1-7), and he was able to catch plenty of fish. All the promises of God in Jesus are Yes and Amen! None of His numerous words has ever failed (I Kings 8:56) because He does not lie (Numbers 23:19, Hebrews 6:18).

Instead of putting all their trust and faith in Jesus Christ, some people usually forget the scriptures and tend to worry unnecessarily by allowing their expectations to weigh them down. (Matthew 6:26-34, Philippians 4:6-7, I Peter 5:6-7). The majority of them are hereby admonished to constantly read Psalm 37:7, which says, *"Be still before the Lord and wait patiently for Him."* Although we must always believe He can do it (Matthew 9:27-30, Matthew 8:13, Mark 9:23, Luke 1:45, John 11:40), anxiety still seems to weigh some of us down (Proverbs 12:25, 14:30, 17:22).

Our faith must be extremely persistent, like Bartimeus, the blind man (Mark 10:46-52) and the Woman in Matthew 15:22-28. Although Jesus Christ did not want to accede to her request, stating that *"the food that is meant for human beings must not be given to dogs,"* He granted her request nonetheless.

In order to constantly realize that with God, everything shall be possible, we must always bear it in mind that because He rules in the Kingdom of Men (Daniel 4:17), His Will is supreme (Ephesians 1:11, Acts 5:38-39, Daniel 4:35, Psalm 75:6-7).

On some occasions, we may be asking God for something with fasting and prayers; yet nothing seems to be happening. We must not lose hope but ask Him to strengthen us to remain constantly steadfast (Isaiah 40:31, Joshua 1:5-9, 2 Chronicles 16:9, Isaiah 30:15) because the joy of the Lord must always be our strength (Nehemiah 8:10). We must never rely on our own strength (2 Chronicles 26:16, Hosea 10:13, Psalm 52:5-7, 118:8-9, Jeremiah 9:23-24, Jeremiah 17:5), as Jesus Christ admonished us that without Him we can do nothing (John 15:4-5).

Our Heavenly Father has never been in short supply of the needs of man at any point in time (Psalm 145:15-16, James 1:17, Psalm 89:11, 2 Kings 4:1-6, Exodus 16:12-15, Psalm 78:23-29, Exodus 19:5) and Psalm 24:1 clearly confirms this, *"The Earth is the Lord's and the fullness thereof."* Imagine what God did to the children of Israel during their journey through the wilderness for 40 years, when He miraculously did not allow their clothes to tear nor their shoes to become torn (without changing them) according to Deuteronomy 29:5!

We must always be mindful that we cannot force God to do things that He feels we are not yet ready for or cannot yet achieve. This is why we must keep and display a humble spirit before Him at all times, believing that He does not forget the cry of the humble (Psalm 9:12, 25:9, 34:18, Isaiah 57:15, Psalm 147:6, I Peter 5:5).

God knows the right time for us, and once we are persistent in prayer, our requests shall ultimately be met.

5

The Place of Nows, Pledges & Appreciation

As it is with human beings, it is with God, our Heavenly Father. Many of us find it extremely difficult to appreciate and thank God and our fellow human beings for previous acts of goodness to us. Many adults do not see it as necessary or compulsory, not to talk of wanting their children or Wards to imbibe that culture. It could be fatal.

I became addicted to thanking people for anything they did for me as early as eight years of age. This was after having come across the famous account of the 10 Lepers that Jesus Christ healed as documented by the Gospel according to Saint Luke 17:12-19. Though Jesus Christ healed ten Lepers, only one of them returned to say "thank you" and show appreciation to Him. He retorted, *"Were ten of you not healed; where are the remaining nine?"* This means God Himself expects us to always come back and say "thank you for the other day."

Most people are in the habit of saying "don't mention it" whenever someone thanks them for a previous act of favour, goodness or assistance. That phrase is only a lip statement because it hardly ever comes from the heart! Imagine assistance being extended to an individual constantly, without any iota of reciprocal appreciation, while another person shows appreciation regularly, unlike the other person! Between the two of them, who would you be obliged to help more than the other in future? The answer is very obvious because your guess is as good as mine!

I have various examples that I can cite as illustrations to support my line of argument clearly, but I will only refer to one. During my stint in the banking industry, our first Branch Manager was a white man who was fond of buying snacks for us whenever he came back to the office from his lunch break. Unbeknownst to us, he singled out the only staff member among all of us who formed the habit of not saying "thank you" to him whenever he bought something for us! He remained unpromoted for many years. Since I am an inquisitive person, I summoned up the courage to go and meet our Manager and sincerely questioned, "Sir, I noticed that Mr. XYZ seems to be the only person in the branch that has not been promoted for a long time; what is the reason, sir?"

He sat me down and patiently narrated the same scenario that I painted above. He noted that he deliberately withheld his letter of promotion and kept it in his drawer, which he retrieved, explaining that "what is the essence of promoting somebody who could not express appreciation for regular acts of favour?" Although I was baffled, I prostrated with my pair of suits to apologize on his behalf and soon after invited him to the Manager's office to tender profuse apologies. This resulted in the Manager immediately releasing the most current letter of promotion to him! What is the lesson here? *We must cultivate a habit of saying "thank you" before God and man. Our requests and prayers could become impossible to grant if we do not show appreciation for previous deeds or acts of goodness to us. This habitual culture is very paramount!

What about the issue of nows, pledges or promises to God or man; can it hinder our prayers from being answered by God? The very obvious answer is CAPITAL YES!

Without any doubt, if we make a promise to any human being, young or old, the person will indeed dwell on it with the expectation to redeem said promise without talking to God, our Creator. Therefore, the inability to keep promises, vows or pledges could hinder or block our prayers from receiving approval from the throne of Grace or even from man. The scriptures have enough references to back up this claim or posture, as shown below, with a few Golden Verses:

1. **Ecclesiastes 5:4-6** - *"When you make a vow to God, do not delay in paying it, for He has no pleasure in fools. Pay what you vow. It is better that you should not vow, than you should vow and not pay. Let not your mouth lead you to sin, and do not say before the messenger that it was a mistake. Why should God be angry at your voice and destroy the work of your hands?"*
2. **James 5:12** - *"But above all, my brothers, do not swear, either by heaven or by earth or by any other oath, but let your "yes" be yes, and your "no" be no, so that you may not fall under condemnation.*
3. **Deuteronomy 23:21-23** - *"If you make a vow to the Lord your God, you shall not delay in fulfilling it, for the Lord your God will surely require it of you, and you will be guilty of sin. But if you refrain from vowing, you will not be guilty of sin."*
4. **Numbers 30:2** - *"If a man makes a vow to the Lord, or swears an oath to bind himself by a pledge, he shall not break his word. He shall do according to all that proceeds out of his mouth."*
5. **Psalm 61:8** - *"So will I ever sing praises to your name, as I perform my vows day after day."*
6. **Psalm 76:11** - *"Make your vows to the Lord your God and perform them; let all around Him bring gifts to Him, who is to be feared."*

7. **Job 22:27** - *"You will make your prayers to Him, and He will hear you, and you will pay your vows."*

Other relevant scriptures are Matthew 5:33-37, Leviticus 5:4-13, Proverbs 20:25, Psalm 66:13, I Samuel 1:11, Psalm 66:14, Psalm 56:12, Psalm 116:14-19, Genesis 28:20-22, Nahum 1:5, Psalm 50:15, Judges 11:29-40, Numbers 29:39, 2 Samuel 15:8 and the last one which I wish to quote is Jonah 2:9, *"But I, with the voice of thanksgiving, will sacrifice to you, what I have vowed I will pay. Salvation belongs to the Lord."*

From all of the above, although God did not expressly declare that He would not answer our prayers for refusing to redeem our vows or pledges, it is implied that such postures by us could debar and impede our prayers from being answered.

6

Sin, the Master Stopper!

This book would be virtually "worthless" if I failed to discuss the impact of sin on our daily lives; and, by implication, the negative effect it would have and act as a strong barrier to our prayer requests from God!

Everybody knows the difference between good and bad. We all know that if a parent has two children and only one of them constantly does the will of the Parent, such a child will always be in the Parents' good books. That's exactly how we are before and in the sight of God, without any equivocation.

Thus, from our discussions so far, we've made many attempts to confirm that nothing is absolutely difficult for God to do. However, we must also emphasize that sin could be a significant stumbling block to our prayer requests. It is like a plague before our Almighty Father because He openly hates it. This fact is buttressed by Psalm 66:18, which says, *"If I regard iniquity in my heart, the Lord will not hear me."*

One can write pages upon pages on this aspect of this book, but the most essential take-home points are as explained hereunder:

1. God created the ten (10) Commandments for our benefit, to make our living a comfortable one, not necessarily for Himself. A cursory look at the contents of the Commandments would show that half of them deal with our relationship with our fellow human beings, while the other half bind us with our God! Has this ever occurred to you?
2. The first book of the Bible (also known as the book of Moses) tells us in **Genesis 1:28**, *"And God blessed them, and God said to them, be fruitful and multiply, and replenish the earth and subdue it and have dominion over the fish of the sea and over the fowl of the air, and over every living thing that moveth upon the Earth."* As beautiful, promising and convincing as the above may seem, it could be extremely difficult, if not totally impossible, for some people to key into and claim that Divine provision or promise if we indulge in sin.

Therefore, it will be in our best interest to critically examine our daily ways of life to see how we can unbundle our lives from a sinful triangle; and begin to have a convincing heart that abides by God's tenets, rules, and Commandments.

Many of us do unto others what we would never expect the other to do for us! We openly cheat others while we feel glaringly offended whenever we are cheated. We do unto others what we obviously cannot condone in the minutest form.

As Believers and as true Children of God, nobody can ever score 100% before God when it comes to how we live our lives, but we can constantly strive to be upright in our daily activities to live right and be righteous in His sight.

While growing up, I remembered almost daily God's commandments as set forth in Exodus 20:3-26, which serve as a guide for our daily lives. But in reality, how many of us really strive as much as possible to comply with them, line by line, without default in one area or the other? It is high time we began to allow those Laws to thoroughly guide our daily transactions with God and over fellow human beings. After all, it is for our own comfort, convenience and most importantly, there to ensure that nothing shall be impossible for us to achieve in our daily activities.

7

Family Generational Curses

A very good and relevant corollary to the previous chapter is the issue of generational influence! The Bible is explicitly clear on this according to Exodus 34:7 *"God will visit the iniquity of the fathers on the Children and the Children's children, to the third and the fourth generation."* We can find that in the Old Testament, and even in the New Testament, Romans Chapters 5-7, Apostle Paul tells us that from a certain point of view, human sin and death are a corporate problem rather than an individual one. He tells us that *"one man's sin (Adam) brought guilt to all people"* (Romans 5:18) and that sin entered the world because one man sinned, and death came because of sin (Romans 5:12).

That is why each one of us remains a *"slave of sin"* unless we are set free by the redemptive Blood of Jesus Christ. (Romans 6:20-22) Thus, in order to get out from under the generational curse, we have to be grafted into a NEW family tree through Eternal Salvation. (Romans 11:11-24)

As Believers, we know that there is only one standard God uses to judge the world and determine the saved from the unsaved: faith in Jesus Christ of Nazareth. The scripture confirms this in I John 5:12 thus, *"Whosoever has the Son has life; whosoever does not have the Son of God does not have life."*

"For God did not send His Son into the world to condemn the world, but that the world through Him might be saved. He who believes in Him is not condemned, but he who does not believe is condemned already because he has not believed in the Name of the only begotten Son of God" (John 3:17-18). The Old Testament Prophet Jeremiah wrote 600 years before the birth of Jesus Christ, and he anticipated this New Testament perspective that ultimately, everyone will answer for their own actions.

8

The Golden Steps to Answered Prayers

In conclusion, and to briefly summarize the essence of this book, permit me to state as follows categorically:

1. **Nothing under the Sun is too difficult for God to do for us.**
2. **We must never pray or ask amiss.** (James 4:3-4)
3. **We must live according to God's Commandments.**
4. **We must always pray in the Name of Jesus Christ of Nazareth.** (Philippians 2:9-11)
5. **It is compulsory to employ God's Words to back up and propel our prayer requests.**
6. **Our requests to God must not be for selfish purposes.**
7. **We must ask Him with a humble spirit.**
8. **Sin is always a clog in the way of our prayers; always remember, pray against generational curses.**
9. **It is extremely essential to redeem all of our vows and pledges to God.** (Ecclesiastes 5:4-6)

10. **Learn to say "thank you", for the other day, to God and man.** In other words, we must constantly appreciate God for previous deeds, which would ultimately encourage Him to do more for us . (Luke 17:12-19)

If you found wisdom in this book, I encourage you to buy as many copies as possible for your friends and loved ones. Not only that, please follow all the teachings so that nothing shall be impossible for you to receive from God. May God continue always to grant us our heart's desires, Amen.

A Sinner's Prayer

Dear Heavenly Father,

I come to You in the Name of Jesus Christ.

You said in Your Word, "Whosoever shall call upon the name of the Lord shall be saved" (Romans 10:13). I am calling on Your Name, so I know You have saved me now.

You also said that "if you confess with your mouth the Lord Jesus and believe in your heart that God has raised Him from the dead, you will be saved. For with the heart one believes unto righteousness, and with the mouth, confession is made unto salvation" (Romans 10:9-10). I believe in my heart Jesus Christ is the Son of God. I believe that He was raised from the dead for my justification, and I confess Him now as my Lord and Savior.

Thank you, Lord, because now, I am saved!

Thank You, Lord, because I know you have heard my prayer. Thank You, Lord, because I am now born again.

Signed _____

Date _____

About the Author

Apostle Dr. Victor Adekunle Adewusi was a passionate Spiritual Leader and Father of many children and grandchildren.

He was also the Author of five books *"The Secrets of Happy Parenting," "Control Your Anger," "Praise, Appreciation & Thanksgiving (PAT)," "Mine Shall Be Done,"* and *"Fear Not, Cheer Up, Do Not Despair."*

Until his passing, he was the General Overseer of The Eternal Sacred Order of The Cherubim and Seraphim Church, Oke Ibukun Branco; The Governor of the Yabatech Class of 1986 governing council; a Member of The Chartered Institute of Management; A Fellow of The Chartered Institute of Taxation of Nigeria and A Fellow of The Institute of Chartered Accountants of Nigeria (ICAN).

Apostle Dr. Victor Adekunle, who was a philanthropist, has drawn on his personal breakthrough life experiences to help people overcome challenges and attain greater achievements in their life.

www.ingramcontent.com/pod-product-compliance
Lightning Source LLC
Chambersburg PA
CBHW070342010526
44107CB00004B/594